"Sometimes a force of nature meets a poet of equal power... meditations are composed of cycles incorporating the sacred lunar number thirteen, a meditative lyric of survival that becomes a chilling testimony: '...the only significant light that New Orleans would experience after sundown came from the moon...' Dave Brinks is a New Orleans poet that commands our full attention."
— Maureen Owen

"Dave Brinks' The Caveat Onus is a serial work in verse which beautifully demonstrates the poet's mind, heart, poetic skill and grace—a remarkable opus with its roots in Brinks' well developed sense of humor and creative play. The Flood struck New Orleans while Brinks was composing his cycle of poems. This is a thrilling work of the imagination, lucid and rhythmically compelling."
— John Sinclair

"Deeply conceived, methodically executed, these poems erect a luminous bridge between the personal and the social, the mystical and the mundane. We hear labor pains and witness the joys of birth, even as the moonlight falls upon the waters of a Katrina-submerged New Orleans. Here is Dave Brinks as poet and priest, myth-maker and raconteur. The Caveat Onus is, truly, a 'golden book of words.'"
— Niyi Osundare

"'Today the paper writes the tree,' as Dave Brinks notes in The Caveat Onus, an interconnected sequence of some 169 thirteen-line meditations. It's true about the paper in these meditations that present themselves as totemic explorations of what Robert Duncan might term the 'noumenal' notifications of verse. Some of the most powerful of Brinks' meditations trace the spiritual topology of New Orleans and the unearned suffering during and after the Great Storm of 2005."
— Ed Sanders

"Throughout this luminous and remarkable work, The Caveat Onus, the poet Dave Brinks writes of the devastation of his beloved city New Orleans, and of what remains; the people he loves, the ruins of the city, and of the future whose story is yet to be told."
— Brenda Coultas

"Dave Brinks' book of poetic meditations, The Caveat Onus, *bravely shoulders the dual burdens of its occult/surrealist compositional matrix and the actual circumstances of recent life experience in his home town, the great city of New Orleans. It succeeds in making the reader engage with the musical pleasures of the text while also aware of the quiet background drumbeat of tragedy and joy.*"   *– Anselm Hollo*

"*What is so amazing amidst all this dazzling and poignant poetry is the elegant precision of its underpinnings, its formal and iconographic shapes, guides, and references. It is totally original, brilliantly written, and so, so moving and interesting. What a truly amazing lopus, conceptually rich, meticulously shaped, an epic...*"   *– Moira Roth*

"*David Brinks is evidently one of the saints of poetry, like a young Francis Steloff in her shop or Louise Solano at the Grolier. The sufferings are now accurately transcribed in* The Caveat Onus *as elegies to a city that he hopes will revive. None of us know anything but the truth of his rage. His poems are illustrations of a coffin lost beside the river. His work is as big as a city and as intimate as the improvisations of an action muralist. After the floodwaters, comes the response of a poet: total commitment, Cagean devotion to poetry and the city of trouble and music.*"   *– David Shapiro*

"The Caveat Onus *poems are depositions of particulates. I found myself ultrasounded by totem animals, and sifted through macro/micro matrices. Dave Brinks' cosmic fluid/flow poetry, flash flooded by the tragic atmospheric condition of hurricane Katrina, is a metamorphic experience in which the poems archive themselves in the body.*"   *– Nicole Peyrafitte*

"*Hallucination, dream, nightmare, meditation—Dave Brinks'* The Caveat Onus *arrives with a post-Katrina, post-apocalyptic New Orleans tragedy. From this ancient tune, Brinks makes use, as poetry must, of all available wisdom to engage us.* The Caveat Onus *comes forward to help show us a way onward for a city and a nation in peril.*"   *– Hank Lazer*

"The Caveat Onus: Book One *is an act of love, a testament to Dave Brinks' respect for craft, invention, and humanity. Spun from lunar cycles, the poems here constitute the first stage of a reader's enlightenment about the 'Cave at Onus' or the obligatory habitation of post-Katrina languages. By clever placement and displacement of language, Brinks offers us meditations that focus and transform our engagement with poetry. The poems heighten our sense of Brinks' aesthetic of necessity, his determination to give us twenty-first century moments of recognition. Under the influence of* The Caveat Onus *we move from anger and anxiety into proximities of accept-ance, and the mindscape of intimate estrangement. As moments both of recognition and recovery, this work offers essentials for healing. Brinks knows that water must enter a reader before the reader enters the water. Let* The Caveat Onus *enter you.*"
                                                        – Jerry W. Ward

"*In* The Caveat Onus, *Dave Brinks discovers a wild and unhinged environment. The heart and head of these poems are totally on the ground. His is a vision of loving anarchy and goodness born of the stuff of everyday giddy-up. He is a true original.*"   *– Peter Gizzi*

"*I think it was one of the Daltons, before taking the Northfield bank, who, seeing a motor car on the main thoroughfare, said, 'it's a wonderment.' You, Dave, are a wonderment.*"   *– Bill Berkson*

"*Dave, you're a Gold Mine!*"   *– Lawrence Ferlinghetti*

"*First, look up in perfect silence at the stars, then read this book.*"
                                                        – Bernadette Mayer

The Caveat Onus

meditations

DAVE BRINKS

Boston, MA

THE CAVEAT ONUS: Meditations ©2009 Dave Brinks. Black Widow Press edition ©2009. Originally published as four separate books by Lavender Ink.

Black Widow Press is an imprint of Commonwealth Books, Inc., Boston, MA. Distributed to the trade by NBN (National Book Network) throughout North America, Canada, and the U.K. All Black Widow Press books are printed on acid-free paper. Black Widow Press and its logo are registered trademarks of Commonwealth Books, Inc.

Joseph S. Phillips and Susan J. Wood, PhD., Publishers
www.blackwidowpress.com

Book and Cover Design: Kerrie Kemperman
Cover and Interior Photographs: iStock and Shutterstock, respectively

ISBN-13: 978-0-9818088-4-0
ISBN-10: 0-9818088-4-0

Library of Congress Cataloging-in-Publication Data on file

Brinks, Dave, 1967–

Printed by BookMobile

10 9 8 7 6 5 4 3 2 1

The Caveat Onus

meditations

DAVE BRINKS

for Mina and Blaise

Acknowledgements

The author gratefully acknowledges those editors who generously featured sections of this work in their literary journals, magazines and anthologies: *Breaking Ground, Callaloo, Constance, Exquisite Corpse, Kulture Vulture, La Reata, Lungfull, New Laurel Review, New Orleans Review, Not Enough Night, Now Culture, Origin, Saw, State of the Union, St. Mark's Poetry Project Newsletter, Tool, Trumpet, Xavier Review*, and *Yawp: A Journal of Poetry & Art*.

The author extends his dearest gratitude to poet Bill Lavender who published *The Caveat Onus* in four prior volumes: *Book One, Book Two, Book Three,* and *Coda* through Lavender Ink.

The author bows gracefully to the Krewe of Black Widow Press, and its Capitan, Joe Phillips, for bringing these four volumes together as one.

The author reserves his deepest appreciation for Megan Burns, and for the great people of New Orleans, and for his extended family of friends, artists, and poets far and near.

ONWARD!

Table of Contents

Totem
pole
animals

13 -
moons
of
Mayan
calendar

Publisher's Note:

Black Widow Press would like to thank Bill Lavender of Lavender Ink (and now also head of the University of New Orleans Press) for allowing us to consolidate the four books of *The Caveat Onus* into one unified whole. *The Caveat Onus* is but one of many fine books that Bill's sharp eye and poetic sense have helped bring to life over the years in New Orleans. The city itself is seeing an explosion of activity in the arts as young people and artists of all backgrounds and mediums continue to move into the city post-Katrina. Amidst the rebuilding and the perpetual decay of this atmospheric and improbable city these artists, writers, poets, and musicians are adding a level of energy and excitement to the city that is impossible to find in most large cities let alone a city of the modest size of New Orleans. So many artists in all fields are combining efforts, events, and creations that one is tempted to think of Breton's concept of "convulsive beauty" as the juxtapositions and energy work to create, in New Orleans, "new" art in all sense of the word. Perhaps, because of the flood, the destruction of much of the city, yet leaving enough of it intact to build upon, New Orleans is similar to the half destroyed European cities after the wars: a time of confusion, yet also of opportunity and artistic upheaval where rules are abandoned and petty allegiances no longer matter. Think of the new and major artistic movements that were born in the distressed cities throughout Europe, especially after WWI. Perhaps we are witnessing first hand the same type of artistic rebirth, the right ingredients all thrown together into an artistic gumbo, that is causing this very visible outpouring of energy that is tangible and can be felt throughout the city.

For poetry in New Orleans, Dave Brinks is at the epicenter. It would be enough to be an outstanding poet, but he is also an integral part of the whole scene. He edits *YAWP: A Journal of Poetry & Art*, is a co-founder of the New Orleans School for the Imagination, publisher/editor of Trembling Pillow Press, and operates one of the best poetry venues anywhere, the infamous Gold Mine Saloon, on Dauphine Street in the French Quarter. He is one of the people who are truly contributing towards this great artistic and convulsive rebirth of this city, a city that I have loved since first stumbling into the Quarter in 1988. Black Widow Press is pleased to bring out this one volume edition of *The Caveat Onus*, a series of books I first read a couple of years ago and immediately had to read again, think about, and then obsess that it needed to all flow from one volume instead of the four it eventually became as it unfolded after Katrina.

Joseph Phillips
Black Widow Press
Boston & New Orleans

for which silential grief shall we choose to be the drum
and by whom mounted
by what triumphant heel
toward the strange bayous

Aimé Césaire
from *Merciless Great Blood*

Book One

bat

one

stared into
everwhich at everwhat
this slender hour comes forward
barefoot to the sun
if only I had gray green
black brown yellow eyes
or a door I could see
through terribly clearly
slowly the answer
becomes an epitaph
a flip of the coin
juggling apples
tracing hexagrams

two

O tough assed angels
deadly reckoners of cheap promises
guardians to the gates of no paradise
and bohemeths that cometh
like Whitman oversized comets
landing in City Park lagoon
ordered me to be made
and while more than once
I gazed at my feet
more than the heavens
and more true *I said yes*
having done many things
but never against you

three

words of the koan
ho-hum like eiderdown
my eyes have the patience of sleep
a loveless faith to love itself
and as I am no more
happy than happy
—> eventually there are days
I can't know anything
to which of you is not meadow
smelling faintly of heather
the breath of a young girl
mouth open
going to the sun

four

I observed my fingers
never knowing when to stop
because of an abeyance of light
because of my desire
to please you
but to go on forever
to say I have a million thoughts
to steal chocolate
or what a lack
of seriousness might mean
the apparatus can then answer
in straight sentences
I write to kill time

five

for Bernadette Mayer

dear Bernadette your books
are an act of chaos
they know so much
about pinecones
and like the fireflies
that visit your front porch
—> most Julys
or that recipe for wild carrot
soup we've sometimes
planned our days around
you're a good
example of everything
I've loved

six

I should not know how artfully
you can love me
just past sunset
the staghorn sumac sings
all night
acacia leaves make
our conversations witty
occasionally I'll come to a path
that leaves in all directions
at its center is a form
of story-telling
a kind of ceremony latin
that comes from moving

seven

on December 22 1978
the calendar of lucky and unlucky days
paints my head
who only glances at you
far from any brazen sea
every husbanded history
—> like the constellation Sanguinaris
where the plants
get planted watered
and whited out
I dream a lot to write it down
like black holes on the ergosphere
of memory

eight

as little as one needs to survive
vital statistics are never
a cure for food poisoning
they come from studying hunger
maybe someday I'll
have a big garden
I'll wear it like a beautiful necklace
of asparagus tips and avocado
and deep in winter's
accumulation of night
in a coloring book
you'll talk as lightly as you can
from the golden book of words

nine

for Philip Lamantia

the blood of the air
the scimitars of antediluvian wastes
are going home from work now
traveled by light beams
gleaming with lizard paint
ectoplasms whose galaxies you've exhaled
→ this is the grey limit
ad astra ad astra
but for love and Ornithos
of wandering sound
death is a pineapple
those Colma landscapes
crossing over then seen

ten

I could spend hours
just staring at the cemetery
heaps of stone
a can of bones (lived-in)
out of this dead city
you carved yourself free and awoke
—> only The Horse knows why
on the heat of the bed
as like life by name
ambiguity of course
or the angels that surround us
everything that begins
from a child's song toward feeling

eleven

love leads me by the nose
of my birth
a stubble of hair
the 5am of birds
caterpillars falling from the trees
a roach scooching
⟶ on its back
across the front porch
whichever comes first
like the instruction manual
for that little red wagon
I put together
yesterday with Mina

twelve

to glimpse and to glide
it's better than a padded room
though I'm never sure
how to feel when I'm awake
will you meet me
smiling on the west wind
I'm always a little disappointed
when my pillow hits the floor
it's like that comeuppance
that arrives with summer
when mosquitoes are waiting
outside the back door
some mornings are full of no noise

thirteen

for Daniel Finnigan

I know as much
about the past and future
as a man on a dark street corner
holding a blade
but just outside the city
scratching my head
—> I'm a fish lying on its back
beside a clear stream
how easily contentment
comes to a single leaf
whose appearance
was once always
only outwardly green

scorpion

fourteen

the horizon was suddenly
of clay
the myrtle green
in her green eyes
passed through his mouth
her voice was the law
of involuntary years
sweet as oboe & musk
he dreams she will become an accordion
dipped in blue
she dreams of all the foetid
masses dipped in blue
a silence existing between two words

fifteen

for Pierre Joris and Nicole Peyrafitte

in a taxi or an old shoe
what you are and what you do
who would guess
there's some kind of luck
that chooses
the pure filth of devotion
→ this book isn't reading itself
I start to mutter a sandwich
and dream of my high priestess' toes
she dreams with a lisp
and for all the fish
sleeping at the bottom
of the ocean

sixteen

broke upon buttons and seams
for his trumpet
for his lute
he saw his whole being
beginning to form
the fleshy balloon of a head
—> deeps of cloudless green
C for the calliope of love
houses with the encryption of an X
and the sun and smell
of standing rivers
"unsewerable defecations"
waiting as evidence

seventeen

the blind goddess spins us on a wheel
with a finger to her lips
holding back a secret
that shouldn't be known
today it's a circus musical
a soundtrack with violins
→ burbling & gloated
a religion with a faceless moustache
kept in place with slop glue
a busted hourglass whose operations
have been reduced to one
to force the head down
and make the knees bleed

eighteen

in this visage not death
I wouldn't hesitate to say goodbye
as I would to you
sounding like a person
I can't defeat
but for the terrible voyeur in a dark-room
—> the clock the monkey the moonshine
it's like putting bricks on jell-o
the sound blurs
and leaves the throat
clogging the circuitry
to be completely
just a kiss

nineteen

crayons were a start
horses gave me an education
as did the belly-buttons
I discovered as a child
that's why the ferris wheel can
become a bicycle if it wants to
ah the ewe of possibilities
direct premonitions
this morning a patch of dense sunlight
is opening up the floor
I have a vertical memory
and like the dancing cartoon I am
it stands from head to toe

twenty

you feel perfectly happy
when flowers
are on the table
but now that
what is left of night
drifts slowly
—> back to the lake
how to say the drowning
city of New Orleans
I will never
forgive America
for tying bodies to streetlamps
so they won't float away

twenty-one

for Romano Zamprioli

here I am
turned thirty-eight this year
regno sopra fantasmi
who sleeps with his head
in front of his eyes
and like any other cloud
⟶ or sun staring
back over water
flowing heartless
and green
I offer a kernel of darnel
from the tongue
of an old child

twenty-two

I am a creature of anonymous tableau
my journey to the desert
was spent in town
on expensive wine
I thought I was heir
to the great bedroom door
—> but to see the aurora of your eyes
gone from brown to blue
it was the wish that wasn't wished for
today I blot out those
dreams and pretend
I'm counting this morning's oranges
in a fruit bowl

twenty-three

beneath the veil of perfect meaning
fantastic tortoises
held out their arms like wings
then came the armies of tumbling water
giving birth to grey grass
where I no longer go
—> it'll take me 300 years to remember
that afternoon
what it was to ascend a staircase
whose only escape was face down
and whereafter we walked
recounting the stories to our children
the reasons no one came

twenty-four

thanks to the ruins
the things in my house
are barely recognizable
and can be found in a landfill
near Almonaster Boulevard
today I'm wearing
⟶ a new pair of shoes
ones that can't remember
where I've been
only my feet know better
and besides that
I've got a bigger problem
the rest of me remembers more

twenty-five

from porch to porch
the waters rise
finally to rest on Canal Street
then comes the floatable mattress
the shoe box the grocery basket
the stuffed animal toys
→ it doesn't have to make sense
but in the geometry of the mind
for one billionth of a second
you hold a photograph
touching the face
where the eyes are
and everything does

twenty-six

for Jerry W. Ward, Jr.

imagine this city and no one in it
little paths of lake and river
where sunflowers sprout
from the scales of dying fish
how the mood of that
forms two halves of a prayer
→ next Sunday is Christmas
and Gray Line bus passengers
are paying $35 to see the devastation
is this supposed to be
the happiest moment of our lives
O Felicity you can't have it both ways
I don't care what street it is

deer

twenty-seven

for Jonathan Kline

if whats were ifs
and paradise was open daily
then storytime could slip
into something more comfortable
like a pair of chopsticks
to hold up your hair
$\longrightarrow$ sailing west over the Bodhi tree
dropping coins
into the blue
of Lake Michigan
and but for the clock's pendulum
capable of the debut
of everything you despise

twenty-eight

I am painting yellow
from a second story window on Dauphine
but everything is so green
like the little cross atop the church
on Jackson Square
what a great excuse for the eyes
—> to pretend everything has a purpose
I'm moving toward
a more self-destructive solution
first the stars then the moon
this time the damage
is going to be more than perfect
blue is the most difficult color to use

twenty-nine

are you a hyperborean
hyperboreans are people who live
in a northern paradise
of perpetual sunshine beyond
the reaches of god and
the north wind
—> they're also ancestors
to their modern day counterparts
who suffer from cold
platitudes like oil drilling
which morphs refuge into refuse
and makes life miserable
for the caribou

thirty

for Gina Ferrara

Texas was a bit of a surprise
that Katrina or Rita
didn't end up there
with shovels and scoops
on front loaders to dig them out
from the years & sadnesses
that lay ahead
slabs of concrete
where chairs once sat
looking up at the blackboard
just another day
like the landfills reopening
which were already condemned

thirty-one

to glimpse and to glide
it's better than a padded room
though I'm never sure
how to feel when I'm awake
driving down a street full of no noise
it's like that comeuppance
—> that arrives one night
months after the storm
Megan & I get out the car
and see the sky over New Orleans
replaced by a giant circle
with a line running through it
and the only thing left is the moon

thirty-two

I'm alternately traveling
to the other universe
where our house is perfectly
undamaged by the scum lines
from Lake Pontchartrain
it's a place full of archangel leftovers
—> the cat's pajamas
my vaudevillian hammer
my empty can
of Zarathustrian silly-string
if only my Methuselah had wings
it's a kind of love
that can never be unmade

thirty-three

sometimes the universe is a jumble
only I know about
and when it flaps its wings
according to what it thinks
I play court to no heaven
the blameless sky
—> the flowers' no flowers
nor the lashing of the drums
and dream my way forward
until the clock's hands
spin in both directions
where water comes from water
and the lotus is lotusing

thirty-four

not all of the schools of the brain
have my prompt attention
it's like that story out of Genesis
where knowledge is measured
by a tongue-shaped kiss
and that's how they found me
$\longrightarrow$ the serpent coiled thrice around my neck
I could feel her licking my eyeballs
beside a half-glimpsed waterfall
each second canceling out the next
like a deliciously cored apple
its leftover shavings
encircling the mouth and chin

thirty-five

it's a trick to follow my lover's eyes
the architecture of her body
was not just meant to inspire
such is the palate this morning
where half sounds
become half silences
—> until the ancient practice
of shifting pillows
finds the right spot
later she'll attempt a handstand
from the bed to the floor
where nothing but
the traditional polka will do

thirty-six

the apartment seems to be getting smaller
used books can never leave my head
and Blaise Cage is
about to set foot into the world
if he's anything like our Mina
it'll be another great trip to the jungle
→ I'll hear monkeys
as "Tongo" crosses his knees
and does a quick somersault
from his mama's belly
and by the light of her omnipresent smile
he'll never be more famous
than the day he was born

thirty-seven

for Moira Roth

my eyes are a strange building
my astronomy can be found in a courtyard
gardening the moon
it's like that game I played
when I was a kid
where the mirrors inside telescopes
→ made weird shapes appear in my head
and I knew I'd never get lost
because wherever lost was
I was sailing past the Isle of Tenderness
scratching my belly
on my way to the invisible gates
of wooden Troys

thirty-eight

the sky of January is not blue
and I feel like all of my ruling planets
have turned against me
so I'm painting myself out of the picture
to include anything that doesn't include
hurting myself or anyone else
—> it's like that moment when laughter starts
following you around like a baboon of despair
O Maelstrom of Maelstroms & Abominations
you've transformed the city of New Orleans
into a busted-face emotion no one can explain
and like the watermelons of St. Bernard
it's hard trying to pretend the waters never came

thirty-nine

I live in a tree in the shape of a house
where nothing has a schedule
like the table on the front porch
where I pull up my chair
and watch the silence of 4am
fill up with birds
—> but today I'm just visiting
like the time I came by boat with my uncle
to see what could be salvaged
why I brought a camera that day I'll never know
no eyes will ever understand the pictures in my mind
of all the flowers & coffins near the railroad tracks
floated out of their tombs

owl

forty

I gazed at my feet
smiling on the west wind
deeps of cloudless green
gone from brown to blue
how the mood of that
does a quick somersault
—> from the bed to the floor
I play court to no heaven
looking up at the blackboard
tracing hexagrams
to say I have a million thoughts
a loveless faith to love itself
who only glances at you

forty-one

her voice was the law
that chooses
the fleshy balloon of a head
today it's a circus musical
I can't defeat
first the stars then the moon
→ where water comes from water
slowly the answer
fills up with birds
I'll wear it like a beautiful necklace
to pretend everything has a purpose
occasionally I'll come to a path
where I no longer go

forty-two

for Niyi Osundare

this slender hour comes forward
to see what can be salvaged
the flowers' no flowers
how to say the drowning city of New Orleans
each second canceling out the next
such is the palate this morning
—> what it was to ascend a staircase
of wandering sound
but to go on forever
where nothing has a schedule
I dream a lot to write it down
a busted hourglass whose operations
ordered me to be made

forty-three

you carved yourself free and awoke
in straight sentences
sounding like a person
landing in City Park lagoon
it's like that moment when laughter starts
never knowing when to stop
and whereafter we walked
months after the storm
finally to rest on Canal Street
the blameless sky
as little as one needs to survive
I have a vertical memory
that comes from moving

forty-four

eventually there are days
stared into
just past sunset
far from any brazen sea
heaps of stone
sweet as oboe & musk
—> and like any other cloud
how easily contentment
leaves the throat
gardening the moon
from a second story window on Dauphine
it's a place full of archangel leftovers
the sky of January is not blue

forty-five

for Jerome and Diane Rothenberg

ah the ewe of possibilities
I'm a fish lying on its back
beside a clear stream
fantastic tortoises held out their arms like wings
horses gave me an education
a religion with a faceless moustache
kept in place with slop glue
I start to mutter a sandwich
whichever comes first
the clock the monkey the moonshine
ectoplasms whose galaxies you've exhaled
I am a creature of anonymous tableau
ho-hum like eiderdown

forty-six

for Andrei Codrescu

the cave at onus
is actually a place
I've been there many times
it's kind of like the poor man's
oracle at Delphi
a voice speaks to you
→ from oblivion
whose mouths are zero-shaped
and all in the key of blue
before entering you'll be asked to drink
from the headwaters of that loneliness
where silence becomes a song
ending with the mind of an owl

forty-seven

I'm moving toward
a silence existing between two words
I don't care what street it is
and like the fireflies
beneath the veil of perfect meaning
my journey to the desert
is opening up the floor
traveled by light beams
will you meet me
in this visage not death
clogging the circuitry
who would guess
my astronomy can be found in a courtyard

forty-eight

to be completely
like black holes on the ergosphere
for one billionth of a second
ad astra ad astra
forms two halves of a prayer
until the clock's hands
spin in both directions
holding back a secret
C for the calliope of love
a stubble of hair
what you are and what you do
capable of the debut
where I pull up my chair

forty-nine

only The Horse knows why
the staghorn sumac sings
but just outside the city
I could spend hours
driving down a street full of no noise
it's like putting bricks on jell-o
the myrtle green
can never be unmade
Megan & I get out of the car
and by the omnipresent light of her smile
smelling faintly of heather
it doesn't have to make sense
I am painting yellow

fifty

for Rodger Kamenetz

this book isn't reading itself
but now that
no eyes will ever understand the pictures
   in my mind
this is the grey limit
where sunflowers sprout
from the tongue
like the constellation Sanguinaris
little paths of lake and river
today I'm wearing
the blood of the air
the cat's pajamas
what is left of night
that shouldn't be known

fifty-one

my eyes have the patience of sleep
the pure filth of devotion
I know as much
of wooden Troys
beside a half-glimpsed waterfall
to pretend everything has a purpose
—> where half sounds
become half silences
flowing heartless
to force the head down
more than the heavens
sailing west over the Bodhi tree
from the scales of dying fish

fifty-two

I write to kill time
at its center is a form
of memory
touching the face
where the eyes are
like the instruction manual
— > to please you
as like life by name
and bohemeths that cometh
a flip of the coin
crossing over then seen
the horizon was suddenly
outside the back door

Book Two

peacock

fifty-three

I am the aesthetic mirror of bad taste
my mind is made up of birdseed & sorghum
I have a penitent anger
which is well-manicured and egged on
in the frying pan I become
my rococo self
→ I prefer embolisms to metaphor
at the cosmic bazaar I exchange trinkets
with symbolists for self-pity
I have luxurious uses for anything
    taken at random
this question rarely depends
on the definition of love
today the paper writes the tree

fifty-four

for Philip Good

some people have farm animal opinions
I'm only human
in a distant cousin sort of way
my attentions begin
with the puppy dog charm
of an occasional good lick
—> it's a love I can lunch
but to end that way
maybe it's time to take another look
at how the rainbow is achieved
dear sacred members of the bla bla church
my favorite soulless diversions
come from you

fifty-five

I never know which way the day is blessed
what mind would you choose
the one where the roof
sits on the furniture
the freak inscriptions on a white frigidaire
my friend Daniel found a boardgame
    in the street
called *Worst Case Scenario*
I have nothing to set my alarm clock to
the list of "the unidentified missing"
is becoming a puzzle
that slowly unsolves itself
the sun falls into the river
New Orleans was never here

fifty-six

I have a fear of flowers
their anatomy confuses me
the store-bought kind are meant to conjure
a magic one comes to expect
on the steps of a lighted porch
others lead a desperate life in a box
⟶ fastened to the window ledge
of a sixty-floor apartment building
I hope my mind never comes to that
the stakes are stacked against me
finding my way out of a lost beautiful feeling
is something I no longer want
to know how to do

fifty-seven

for Mina

before the water fell
nothing kept us from a good time
it was as simple as digging up
worms in the backyard
trains going by near the playground
were big jaw-droppers
—> the ice cream truck adored us
"the after dinner moonlight wagon ride"
was our most recent ritual
"hopgrassers" "smushrooms" and "puppy
    dog shoes"
were newly minted vocabularies then
now the water keeps falling
it never stops

fifty-eight

for Maureen Owen

it's never a simple matter
to swallow the wrong poison
and ride it out in a room
where there's nothing else to do
if I were in the Himalayas
I'd leave strange tracks in the snow
if I were a great violinist
you'd never know
this concerto is in G sharp
ten thousand thresholds of grey light
are passing through the window
buttoning the flap on my shirt pocket
makes me full cowboy

fifty-nine

today's hallucination
doesn't need me to pinch myself
the problem isn't paranormal
there's an ingrown eyeball
crawling around in the back of my head
that's when I whip out my best home remedies
⟶> like vomiting & pine-flower wine
and if that doesn't help
I hold a lit cigarette to the skin
until it starts to burn
it's just like acupuncture
heaven is a hard climb
I'm just happy to get out of bed

sixty

for Eddie Mac

I'm floating on a stardust channel
behind an eye
that starts from the sublime
then moves in the opposite direction
like the zombie I've become
these recent months
⟶ in a city whose latest *folie de grandeur*
is a blunderfuck called disaster
where the mind never stops seeing double
and the coffin flies keep landing
    on my sandwich
I need a new address for the things in my head
a rare mountain somewhere inside
    a Japanese painting
because what I know no longer seems real

sixty-one

it was one of those meals
that became something more than just soup
like the great talking-monkey
that lives inside our television
delivering his State of the Union address
so we wove it into conversation
—> as one does with dreams
playing leapfrog from one lie to the next
how many 5lb cigars does it take to win
    Capital Hill?
then just before the final standing ovation
I made a trip to the bathroom
and took a bow for democracy
instead of watching it fall on its face

sixty-two

occasionally I feel like the kid
who sees all those terrible things
inside Willy Wonka's
Chocolate Factory
and goes home
and never has anything to say
—> it's like trying to tell Abner Doubleday
you can't handle fastballs
my budding childhood will probably
    never arrive
I'm still too busy
tossing evil wizards wicked witches
and their flying monkeys
off the mountain on my head

sixty-three

for Blaise

we're eleven days into January
and next Tuesday
we're all hoping "Tongo"
comes home from the hospital
with an amazing set of fingers & toes
but whatever special destiny
—> he decides to sing
outside of his mama's belly
it'll be just another reason
scribbled down with invisible ink
and added to my ever-growing list
of why I no longer feel
like the ghost of confused present

sixty-four

my heart is made of honey-pot
sometimes it's a boat
and sometimes it's more than an accident
that's how I learned
Spanish music sounds like clean hair
is your favorite color dirty pigeon too
⟶ it's usually the many-headed ones
that visit me while I sleep
my biggest trouble comes in the daytime
like earlier this morning
when I thought the car in front of me
was dragging an upside down cat
and it turned out to be a white plastic bag

sixty-five

if you rearrange the letters
in Bernadette Mayer
it turns into "bent dream eatery"
mine spells "bard knives"
what a melodious thinking
do you suppose
—> the London Philharmonic will agree
today I'm celebrating the void
with all its invisible o's
some circles are a preamble
to anything we know
like that great wobble that took place
the day Pericles fell to his knees

lizard

sixty-six

I was in my head with sand preparing
for the storm *se soulever*
casting shadow puppets on the wall
jagged instants shaped now to flood proportions
expended motionless
the faucet drips to a destination
—> no one wants to hear
with a word
I start with a line
to be stared at
coming up from the floor
where it finds you
wondering what can account for that sound

sixty-seven

Mina dreamed all the trees were broken
today it's the same sun
but further away
the patio looks like a dried-up aquarium
the weeds are nearly tall enough
a little person might get lost
I'm in there somewhere
tossing a pork chop to a black Cocker Spaniel
Megan's adding mulch to the flowerbed
a toy yellow dump truck
lay on its side near a mud hole
it's a scary familiar
here air there water blue house what floats

sixty-eight

for Herbert Kearney

what was once a street
turns to greet me
the shower curtain the boat propeller
the screen door
busier parts of town
don't seem to remember
the Lower Ninth Ward is still here
an evacuation sign
with its arrow pointing up
where the key fits
who are only sleeping
like the memory of so many
drowned fish

sixty-nine

approaching the end of memory
wakens the anatomy
of dancing a leaf
in your hand
the sudden craving
for more butter & bread
—> my body is shifting gears
death has its own privileges
I give you a picture of feathers
all of these
sleep is temporary
proving what or nowhere
a face toward which I turn & walk

seventy

the entrance to heaven
has its own setbacks
all the doors are jammed and bloodied
there's not a single pair of wings
that match
I ignore the problem and suit-up anyway
—> there's a coronation here
with my name on it
I just need a loving and invisible face
to point me in the right direction
the shape of my hand
takes the form of a shovel
the universe has spoken

seventy-one

for Bill Berkson

O nameless emptiness
the arithmetic is simple
the trees have leaves
the sun has set
at bedtime I lie down for a nap
to know what and why I am
—> if elephants come running
I line up at the watering hole
and refuse to move
between sips
my supper is moonshine
by day I poke along
whispering far away

seventy-two

there's no emergency protocol for today
no obstacle course of floodwaters
    to navigate through
most boats are on sidewalks now
I go on being alive
knowing only what I can know
it's not late August
⟶ I'm waiting to pick up Mina at school
a stream of cars with their headlights on
is leaving a funeral home
in the dark space behind my eyes
it's Convention Center Blvd
there's a mother holding a newborn
saying *he barely wakes up anymore*

seventy-three

for Megan

April is here and all
the trees are newly painted
I want to be a fountain
sparkling with coins
the unavoidable happiness of coming home
lips licking your heels
—> under the bedposts
a duet with Elton John & RuPaul
it's all about relationships
the house has a rectangular design
there's a room for every window
we're moving the furniture around
to get a better view

seventy-four

there must be a self-destruct program
hidden in the belly of my soul
and whenever the universe
wants to get tough with me
someone slips in there
and throws the switch
—> but then maybe
that's my own personal cosmogony
and I'm feeling cross-dimensional again
whatever happens I know two things
my leash has dogs on it
one of them answers to the name Cerberus
and I've been wronged

seventy-five

although the stars don't declare it
the month of Easter is disguised with rabbits
I can see morning
coming off your neck
the emergence of earth from a flower
makes everything new
—> add that to the registry
of notes left on bathroom mirrors
mine is an account
of the clothes I've slept in
now it's the door's turn
to open and close
it's like music to a dog's ear

seventy-six

for Grace Murphy

most human feelings
begin in earnest after dinner
I was forced into a strange position
in an elevator
if God were Picasso
he'd think of the homogenization
⟶ of space
if Picasso were a girl
he might think *what's this rigid form?*
oysters have the ability to change gender too
the menu has me salivating
the ice bucket is graceful
I'm an ice bucket with champagne

seventy-seven

it's never arbitrary to open with a kiss
and come away strange
irises are like that
the orange & purple ones are the easiest to grow
I would be glad to be either
but this is the azure world
—> a city of neighborhoods surrounded by water
that couldn't be turned away
streets where statues of the Blessed Virgin
watch bulldozers roll up
on houses with outstretched arms
even today to the unfamiliar eye
    what couldn't float
remains in a state of fantastic disgrace

seventy-eight

there's this to say about being
at the tail end of a lizard
O delicate death with soft feet
spouting branches over uninhabited playgrounds
O muse of black sand
in the door-yard blooming
—> the welcome night & the stars
let the ghosts of these words
pass from this world
where nothing lives
let our lady of Charon
dress her child in blue
whose sadnesses answer to no name

monkey

seventy-nine

before eerily but often
I've traveled across impossible waters
to see what others
have only thought they've seen
it's like suddenly being able
to pass through a wall
→ in your own home
the structure is still there
but the people have disappeared
and like the notes scribbled down
on the back of my hand
the sidewalks are getting warmer
and have nothing else to do

eighty

some days are best spent
in search of the perfect pinecone
we find my street and paddle down
staring at holes cut in roofs
here comes a little hummingbird
flying at cupolas
Everett & I tie off the boat
to the front porch
it takes a full half hour
for magnolia blossoms to open
on a summer morning
the victims trickling out now are delirious
and some don't know who they are

eighty-one

we're 300 yds from the breach
at the 17th Street Canal
ah the miracles of human engineering
it's like that white plastic daisy
Jonathan planted
in the center of the yard
⟶ after he and Daniel and I threw out
all the gunk in my house
today I can only look down
there aren't any scum lines on this block
an American flag hangs from a tree
the waters that came through here
went past the eaves

eighty-two

for Bill Lavender

tonite the news from the universe
is upstairs in a children's book
in Mina's room
it's almost bedtime
we're making up the words as we go along
the entire animal kingdom
—> applauds this decision
the purpose of meaning is useless
it'll be summer again soon
and like every good magician
whose hands give shape to the invisible
I calibrate my thinking
to accommodate the moon

eighty-three

monkeys and their milk
are a gesture of infinitude
and for all I know
of life en route to *sang d' homme*
that's how my summer should be
at Bernadette & Phil's under the trees
—> Nicole leading us in backyard sing-a-longs
decisions like raspberries or more lawn chairs
there's Simon Peter Brenda Liz Harris
Tom Grace Michael & Pierre
those great chatterers of earth
are a repartee no universe can deny
this boheme fare and its wild air

eighty-four

for Thaddeus Conti

I'm driving down Orleans Ave
not only is my foot falling asleep
the rest of me is having trouble staying awake
so I turn on the radio
and sadly every station I flip to
starts to sound like the soundtrack to my life
—> now I know there's no truth to that
but when I pull into the driveway
it's a pain full of discovery
I see the blue dumpster spilling over
with what's left of the roof
and realize not only is anything possible
it's already happening

eighty-five

walking is pure
if you consider it in reverse
going back through a calendar
on the kitchen wall
to anyplace in New Orleans
before the hurricane entered the gulf
⟶ the leaves of a small oak
sit beside me on the road
in a puddle left by the rains
I'm watching my thoughts lengthen
    into shadows
it's been eight months since we evacuated
I remember thinking I could
hoard more acorns than a squirrel

eighty-six

for Bill Myers

there's a certain challenge
in being human
but not much
if one remembers to
deep in wine
conversations like "The Buddha"
—> and *yeah well what does Wittgenstein know*
about growing up in Wichita KS?
you shift elbows on the bar
and offer a bituminous stare
that's probably as close as I'll get
to the mystery
of your bicycle moustache

eighty-seven

sometime after midnite and by 4am
I unlearn the alphabet
so the mind can enjoy its pleasures
it's like listening to the ocean
cupping water over your dreams
my hands play castles in the sand
—> cephalopods speak to me in Latin or Greek
and as for the acumen of seashells
their stories come full-blown
my eyes pop open on the pillow
trembling raw with brine
the green *dor* of Hypnos exits quietly
then closes the door

eighty-eight

finding a smile on the picture wall
spared by the floodwaters
the roles get reversed
the road is missing
the house is sitting on it
the cars are upside down
—> this is a new equilibrium
the circles around my eyes make larger ones
dawn peels back like a metal enclosure
more water pours through
mushrooming out of storm drains
great chunks of the world lay flattened
the only thing not burning is the river

eighty-nine

for Guy Waltz

there's a peregrination of voices
traveling through my head
everything's moving sideways
starting with the sky
I'm tying my shoes
so they won't come off
downtown in tall buildings
monkey suits are playing cards
with our city's future
we're putting the house back together
this is the rotting gardens of Avalon
a Bali Hai clambake
crawling out from the skunge

ninety

dear body dear heart
there is no sovereign music
or storybook air
starting with a map
that says Lake New Orleans
but to you
—> whose head is bent
in genuflection to the stars
and who will go everywhere
to what end
for the first time
a rendezvous with the hawk
is preening its feathers

ninety-one

once wood tastes water
it never forgets
on our street it's a permanent address
a dead pine still stands
lost in vast shades of ocean
let the reader of these words feel assassinated
and wail mournfully at the sky
louder than numb
transfixed by the moon
ghosts whose faces are my own
I cry for the absence of love
and have no way to send a gift
whose birds have not returned

hawk

ninety-two

my attentions begin
fastened to the window ledge
like the zombie I've become
the one where the roof
lay on its side near a mud hole
there's a coronation here
⟶ expended motionless
the house has a rectangular design
great chunks of the world lay flattened
it'll be summer again soon
today I can only look down
knowing only what I can know
in a puddle left by the rains

ninety-three

for Joshua Walsh

finding my way out of a lost beautiful feeling
the problem isn't paranormal
my heart is made of honey-pot
I hold a lit cigarette to the skin
jagged instances shaped now
    to flood proportions
it's like suddenly being able
to accommodate the moon
the roles get reversed
the circles around my eyes make larger ones
there's a room for every window
here air there water blue house what floats
I'm tying my shoes
lost in vast shades of ocean

ninety-four

this concerto is in G sharp
scribbled down with invisible ink
I have luxurious uses for anything
    taken at random
today I'm celebrating the void
conversations like "The Buddha"
it's like music to a dog's ear
—> but the people have disappeared
my eyes pop open on the pillow
in search of the perfect pinecone
the patio looks like a dried up aquarium
this is a new equilibrium
death has its own privileges
I have nothing to set my alarm clock to

ninety-five

my body is shifting gears
the arithmetic is simple
heaven is a hard climb
I need a new address for the things in my head
an American flag hangs from a tree
the road is missing
there's a mother holding a newborn
add that to the registry
where nothing lives
I'm watching my thoughts lengthen
    into shadows
some days are best spent
deep in wine
starting with the sky

ninety-six

for Linda Hill

it's been eight months since we evacuated
the purpose of meaning is useless
if you consider it in reverse
as one does with dreams
we're making up the words as we go along
the trees are newly painted
spouting branches over uninhabited playgrounds
dear sacred members of the bla bla church
I've traveled across impossible waters
it's not late August
Megan's adding mulch to the flowerbed
my mind is made up of birdseed & sorghum
I never know which way the day is blessed

ninety-seven

for Michael Fedor

sit beside me on the road
where the key fits
on the steps of a lighted porch
before the hurricane entered the gulf
and refuse to move
to know what and why I am
it's like listening to the ocean
on houses with outstretched arms
dawn peels back like a metal enclosure
until it starts to burn
today's hallucination
takes the form of a shovel
a face toward which I turn and walk

ninety-eight

the caveat on us
is a great tear in the dreamwork
forced upon the mind
like a terrible sound
that only compares with silence
where everything belongs to water
—> and whose sadnesses have no equal or worse
O Memory let these creatures stir
snap the teeth of your dragon's snout
send forgetfulness to repair their suffering
the song of the hawk
knows no boundaries
between heaven and earth

ninety-nine

for Paul Chasse

like the ghost of confused present
crawling around in the back of my head
I have a penitent anger
my leash has dogs on it
the sidewalks are getting warmer
there is no sovereign music
—> what mind would you choose
Mina dreamed all the trees were broken
I remember thinking I could
hoard more acorns than a squirrel
this is the rotting gardens of Avalon
the sun falls into the river
New Orleans was never here

one hundred

for Bill Lewin

it takes a full half hour
for magnolia blossoms to open
on a summer morning
if I were in the Himalayas
I'd leave strange tracks in the snow
but this is the azure world
an evacuation sign
with its arrow pointing up
we find my street and paddle down
it's almost bedtime
I unlearn the alphabet
we're putting the house back together
with an amazing set of fingers & toes

one hundred and one

the emergence of earth from a flower
wakes the anatomy
in a distant cousin sort of way
I'm tying my shoes
to the mystery
whose hands give shape to the invisible
dear body dear heart
it's all about relationships
walking is pure
at the cosmic bazaar I exchange trinkets
decisions like raspberries or more lawn chairs
the entrance to heaven
makes me full cowboy

one hundred and two

my hands play castles in the sand
at the 17th Street Canal
it's a pain full of discovery
more water pours through
whose head is bent
in genuflection to the stars
—> this question rarely depends
on the definition of love
the faucet drips to a destination
whispering far away
and as for the acumen of seashells
the entire animal kingdom
their stories come full-blown

one hundred and three

for Elizabeth Garcia

sometime after midnite and by 4am
there's a peregrination of voices
it never stops
everything's moving sideways
the shower curtain the boat propeller
the screen door
—> today it's the same sun
I can see morning
coming off your neck
the trees have leaves
the orange & purple ones are the easiest to grow
and like every good magician
I'm just happy to get out of bed

one hundred and four

starting with a map
I give you a picture of feathers
whose birds have not returned
but to end that way
like a terrible sound
today the paper writes the tree
whose sadnesses answer to no name
mine spells "bard knives"
I go on being alive
playing leapfrog from one lie to the next
the leaves of a small oak
are a gesture of infinitude
on our street it's a permanent address

Book Three

jaguar

one hundred and five

for Michael Ford

I am an uncooked egg
beneath the feathers of a warm bird
comely I came dripping
with the scent of timeless stupid things
monkeys performed
question marks in my eyes
counting back to the hours of my birth
mine is the great lie
of biology that says "I'm alive"
this is what I wished for
the lush the depth of green
a brown line cutting the horizon
four rectangles a busted window the moon

one hundred and six

ordinarily I don't think of clouds
as an obscure emotion
but it's late in the afternoon
my head is resting against a window
   on the plane
I can see myself drawing
in a coloring book
⟶ where I want to live & be
below me is the most hated country in the world
it's like fixing the chain on my first bicycle
or observing fireflies at close range
tonite in New Orleans we'll catch the fireworks
   by the river
I'm spinning the globe on the floor
   in Blaise's room
this is the great period of terror & fear

one hundred and seven

fill your mind with brackish water
lie down in it
stare from rooftops at helicopters
and the burning sun
be advised the dead can't swim
what good does it do
if the tide's going in or out
quiet land where the trees stop moving
impossible human cargo lining the streets
love that went love that never came
it's all over it's not over
tonite I'm amassing an enormous collection
of broken things

one hundred and eight

for Megan

for less than the average day
calmly to face
finally leaving New Orleans
to become a ship
jostled on the waves
what occasions the heart visiting other cities
—> I am bitter at people
walking down the street
talking at tables outside cafes
the couple & their kid just out for a stroll
and what am I doing
I too would like to be someone
other than me

one hundred and nine

it's not easy being near the ocean
the vibe is simple
when you know what water can do
Mina's looking for things washed up in the sand
I'm trying to think sand dollars
and not people
—> my mind feels like a piece of furniture
floating in the hallway
between the ceiling and the floor
it's an important morning lesson
watching her feet march through the surf
earlier I saw lightening at a distance offshore
the horizon has clouds white and blue

one hundred and ten

for Tasha Robbins

I'm surrounded by six-toed pigeons
    & cigarette butts
the wind is slightly at my back
at exactly 10 o'clock
there's a picnic table falling down
and a dog eating grass
I'm not sure who or what it is I love
I'm a nightmare floating b/w New Orleans
    & Washington Sq
even the sound of the nearby fountain
seems to be making its way into my house
but to grow old like that tree
the only difference from this universe
and the one I live in
is a calendar that says August full moon

one hundred and eleven

my yeoman's optimism is on the blink
humans aren't a species
they're an epidemic
and thanks to the geography
of land and mostly water
there isn't any place left to go
so I'm preparing a new set of coordinates
like the silent tick & boom of birds
flying back into the ethers
this isn't an auditory hallucination
it's a prelude to a strange music
heard by the future astronomers
of dusty earth

one hundred and twelve

for Harris Schiff

wherever here is
this is a note of hello
a map that dissolves
as you write something down
I'm counting backwards from infinity
the ostrich the antelope
—> I can't sleep anymore by the window
I think there's been a misunderstanding
about earth
this spaceship has four walls
isn't human proof
and it's beginning to feel like
the results of a bad CAT scan

one hundred and thirteen
for Francis Russell O'Hara

I once ranked high on the registry of stars
none of which I have been able
to lay my hands on
it's something I started doing one day
climbing the water tower
the wind sounded exactly like Stravinsky
the world seemed rounder
and besides knowing what I knew
what's the point of asking
if anything is beautiful or not
I can't help thinking it is
which makes every statement a declaration
to be carried away shining and intact

one hundred and fourteen

a hurricane blows in from the south
a wide flat river sits down in the room
now it's a year later and Mina asks
"When did the storm come?"
"Did it come when you & Mommy were little?"
back in Natchez last September the answers
to our own questions seemed further away
Paul & Beth & Andy & Khaled & I
sat at a table in the Under the Hill Saloon
trying to figure out where the rest
   of our friends were
it was around that time
the days of the week had names
but I couldn't tell you which one it was

one hundred and fifteen

I was listening between friends
from elbow to ear
straining my eyes
birdlike to the last
how many rabbit faces do you see
in a fool moon
⟶ the evening Buddha flickers & reappears
on Warrington Drive near
   the London Ave Canal
beyond a certain point
it's impossible to face a tragedy
the truth is to see
the mind dead on arrival
this is where Bill Lavender saw the flood of sand

one hundred and sixteen

doesn't everyone compile a list
of all the angels that save their ass
today I saw the white pigeon
that hangs out near Burgundy & St. Ann
dodging delivery trucks
baskets of hanging plants dripping
    with hose water
→ another trash pile on the curb
lately I keep dreaming of stairs
that lead down to more stairs
I usually don't behave well
under the influence of religious bondage
tonite a pair of tall transvestites are
making the block

one hundred and seventeen

for The Brocato Family

my eyes are inside a cookie jar
at an Italian ice cream parlor
there's a young couple walking up outside
taking account of their children
this is a song I've waited for
handed-down recipes
Cassata Gelato Panna Cotta Cannoli
all the flavors of unwrapped joy
and just as the hymn
reaches its final refrain
an old man from Palermo
steps gently through the crowd
and holds open the door

dog

one hundred and eighteen

I've become an expert at self-hypnosis
my fingers feel like Edgar Allan Poe
beating time with a coffin lid
sometimes it takes all day
to realize it's not a bad trip
water where the swell says heavy things
——> children calling their mother
stairwell filled with cement chunks & dirt
a pink & purple scooter
put a candle between your eyes
blow the flame out
the storm's been gone a year
and that's a third of my daughter's life

one hundred and nineteen

it's natural & exciting to be alert
the duck quacks
the lizard ambles through leafy cover
the dog chases its tongue
I too am the product of my own
catalog of survival
my vocabulary did this to me
there are no medium-sized emotions
how does your family
spend the afternoon
becalmed or not becalmed
the waves coming up
then sweeping them away

one hundred and twenty

pulled down from a knowledge
whose eye is the moon
there's no need to properly introduce
myself to myself
the moan is in the oak tree's crotch
the watermarks from the storm
———> are nearly invisible now
whether I am alive or not
is no longer a guess
what's your neighborhood look like
born raised and hope to die here
is what most New Orleanians say
and you can see it for miles

one hundred and twenty-one

some say it's the moon
but it's the business of being a person
that messes with my head
I consider myself a ventriloquist of time & space
yesterday the voice on my knee said
I was only five well-built spaceships away
from leaving this planet
O epistemological mind
who can only offer embarrassing solutions
do not disturb my sleepless dreaming
it's much easier to fly through a window
scarifications are an elegant gesture
what shrubbery shall I choose

one hundred and twenty-two
for Simon Pettet

he snags the world with his tongue
it dissolves
he thinks himself more thirsty
his stomach heaves with thirst
he dreams with parched lips
between the shores of two oceans
he is not careful
he staggers onward with his arms out front
drawing a picture of his thirst
as if he were a cloud bursting in air
a dog once familiar to him
finds his body on a dry river bed
and it begins to rain

one hundred and twenty-three

for Lenny Emmanuel

summer goes by simple as a hello
the light entering the holes in my head
seems brighter
I dress myself up in a hammock
   for the afternoon
everything that's gone
goes on from a distance
today I'm staring at childhood pictures
looking for clues
rise up carcass and walk
put on your finest robes
you are a ghost in splendid form
an arithmetic of wind & water
twisting under the trees

one hundred and twenty-four

born from an unnatural scenery
seen from all sides
inside this house without floors or walls
turn in any direction
stand on the front porch
note the crepe myrtles' growth
——> inspect the limbs that are without flower
remove the leaves near both storm drains
for the unobstructed flow of water
retrace your steps
between the sidewalk & the curb
there are only two paths
one is a flatboat passing over my head

one hundred and twenty-five

Sweet William Wild Ginger & Day Lilies
are great conversation starters
they also make good bookmarks
during my visits to the Poetry State Forest
last July I saw two goldfinches
land at Bernadette's bird feeder
—> some people think Bernadette
     is Native American
it's hard not to imagine her house
lit up with fireflies
maybe there's a Walt Whitman in every backyard
that's the sort of thing my mind likes thinking about
and whoever thought to put elephants in birdbaths
is clearly a genius

one hundred and twenty-six

for Ted Berrigan

I am an excursionist
who doesn't need a field guide
to the afterlife
church gives me a mustard feeling
my sleep is reckoned
by the claws of birds
and if my speech sounds untoward at times
it is nevertheless unwavering
for I too have tumbled once or twice
into the briny swamp
having lost my bearings in a "besotted pirogue"
the only paradise I've ever found
lay at the far reaches of elephanthood

one hundred and twenty-seven

the rhythm of the ancient mariner
is an intricate tide
the magician's alphabet
is poured from a cup of wet sand
this castle comes perfectly heart-shaped
and close to the shore
→ letting the water enter from all sides
later I'll settle down for a book & a nap
the first chapter the best chapter
that's when you're on top of the waves
where bathing is legendary
and you can see the little fishes
darting between your legs

one hundred and twenty-eight

I can't keep the rodents in check
not only did they find
our emergency food supply
from last hurricane season
but they're ripping off chunks of cardboard
and building a nest
—> it's obviously a well-planned affair
they've gone through two boxes
and started on a third
we met eye to eye this morning
I can see this is going to be a struggle
there are more of them than there are of me
potato chips & banana cookies
    are their favorites

one hundred and twenty-nine

for David and Lindsay Shapiro

I sing the colostrum the body epileptic
tearing pages from a book
or with tongue
I am also the heave of water
lapping over the back and neck
drawn in by its breath
look on this wonder
swim in it as a sea now consumed
whose gentle white caps
form a puddle at the bottom of my glass
such eyes such pluck such fecund air
I am ready to get on with life
I am already dead

one hundred and thirty
for Nancy Dixon

I am the dog that swallows its tail
I was born under the serpent
and raised in South Louisiana
some people say it looks like a bird's foot
during those weeks following the storm
the only feathered creatures I saw were crows
—> now I'm just glad there's a sky at all
yesterday morning I pointed out Venus to Mina
later we watched two pelicans
crossing the waters of Lake Pontchartrain
water is what gives New Orleans
its crescent shape
but to my mind it's the moon

serpent

one hundred and thirty-one
for Richard Collins

no matter who's doing the counting
if it's a modern calendar
my Mayan pocketwatch says
you're better off tossing yarrow sticks
at the moon
that's why I am here
this hexagram has no margin of error
water can teach you many things
when's the last time
you came home from the ocean
with sand in your shoes
I have no need to exist eternally
infinity x 1 = ZZZzzzz

one hundred and thirty-two

everything happens once many times
like a complicated set of nerves
I was misconceived
does amnesia shape the way you think
consider the sky over New Orleans
in the weeks leading up to the storm
lasciate ogni speranza, voi che vivete
today I'm doing a floor puzzle with Mina
the pieces are the size of my hand
this one looks like a Chinese butterfly
one must guess at a certain loneliness
and if it comes to that
put a stethoscope to my chest

one hundred and thirty-three

this is the geometry of an empty house
a rose lay on the floor of each room
neighbors no longer live next door
or across the street
I have to sit two-dimensionally
and stare for hours
—> as grandchildren & siblings
arrive and walk around
trying to reimagine a future
that's behind them now
the patterns that tea leaves form
at the bottom of my cup
are no help here

one hundred and thirty-four

it's because of the "fixity of contamination"
that my children might not be able
to dig up worms in the backyard
some chemicals in the ground
are not "indigenous" to the soil
which means the latest experiment in "living" is us
—> but let's begin first with laughter
or the disappearance of more wetlands
we owe it to the earth
to give birth to our own version of Atlantis
and besides that what's the difference
between a Hazmat suit and a diving suit
if you can't breath on land

one hundred and thirty-five
for Crystal Kile

show me something new and I'll
begin all over again
with strings and a universe
which doesn't include the historied
embarrassment of man
what I'll do is scribe everything
—> right up to the point
where our ancestors evolve into trees
how much space do you think we'll need
"anything that can happen
is already happening"
and it's the kind of truth
that doesn't require a mistaken identity

one hundred and thirty-six

for Jimmy Ross

the future is not what bothers me
have you ever sent an SOS to yourself
from one universe to the next
I called myself from the Greyhound bus station
to say I had been bitten by The Cosmic Eel
at first I thought it was a practical joke
but the voice sounded like it was in a lot of pain
and when the sarcasm turned to full-out anger
I felt like my own personal crime scene
whatever it was and for very personal reasons
I decided I couldn't be helped
nowadays if the phone rings and it's me
I tell myself I'll be there as fast as I can

one hundred and thirty-seven

this morning here's what I know
there's a whole galaxy
& a half moon in the sky outside
because I woke up and saw it
the universe likes playing ping pong
   with my eyes
and it doesn't matter which team I'm on
the *I Ching* is another game of hide & seek
I'm looking at a picture of John Cage
   looking at me
he says "all answers are answers to all questions"
as ghosted as I am
even when passing through walls
my heart feels like an appendectomy
my brain feels like a bucket of chum

one hundred and thirty-eight

one of the things about vertigo is
you can't flip a coin
then move on with the rest of the day
take the sun for example
put yourself in a tree's shoes
are you sure what the shape of a circle is
—> examine the flesh of your right hand
form a straight line from your mind to the sky
measure it with your feet
count backwards from 0 to 9
this is the tragedy of birth
I have a tendency toward tranquility
let the concert begin

one hundred and thirty-nine

for John Cage

this hexagram has an antenna for a mouth
and the willingness to be pleasantly surprised
I maintain an inevitability
so I can make mistakes
to contradict myself
one for the piano one for the violin
⟶ as for the assailants of this work
I address your admirations with silence
choose any two of them
between half sleeping or half waking
and as softly as possible
without lifting a finger
pound the rice

one hundred and forty

whether there was a storm or not
the circumference of a circle
is hard to undo
I'm moving to a universe
where you don't have to look at the stars
to count them
→ it's like passing through a wormhole
in the trenches of your brain
at night during the day
the news trickles out from a busted chronometer
mine was an improbable education
   not Cambridge
the situation being so vast
thinking mars the page

one hundred and forty-one

for Anselm Hollo

I'm slipping you a note while I can
between disasters
to say I no longer wonder why
we give hurricanes human names
I should have guessed
this was a world I might live in
$\longrightarrow$ here lies earth broadcasting its shadow
to the rest of the universe
cities whose buildings are bent twisted back
   or gone
perhaps all life forms should be placed
under the Witness Protection Program
dear Mr. Keyes you were wrong
"bombs bursting in air" is not a song

one hundred and forty-two

O litterateurs O immortelles
O emporiums of dissected nirvanas
is there something left over from your walking
your moon is cold
and packed for travel like a souvenir
even your stomach digests itself
I should wear sunglasses & plastic gloves
as I lay out your tongue & entrails
and bury them certain fathoms in the sky
let it form a new constellation
I'll even pretend this moment
    doesn't have a name
the acedia of the scribe is a sad trope
O American poesy you disappoint me

one hundred and forty-three

most New Orleanians visit the cemetery
on the Day of the Dead
I'm walking the levee with Megan Mina & Blaise
the Canal Street ferry is pulling away
    from its dock
a barge is making a wide turn downriver
what thoughts do you allow yourself
when the moon is nearly full
my eyes are the kind of water
whose silence reaches for a word to say goodbye
I'm a monkey born like all the others
it's like moving dirt from one hole to another
when I laugh I cry one by one
I sing because I'm outnumbered

rabbit

one hundred and forty-four

I'm counting backwards from infinity
between the shores of two oceans
looking for clues
what's your neighborhood look like
put yourself in a tree's shoes
I think there's been a misunderstanding
⟶> there are only two paths
the duck quacks
from one universe to the next
I have a tendency toward tranquility
let it form a new constellation
walking down the street
whose eye is the moon

one hundred and forty-five

O emporiums of dissected nirvanas
as ghosted as I am
between the sidewalk & the curb
the vibe is simple
there are no medium-sized emotions
the storm's been gone a year
—> I'm not sure who or what it is I love
I am bitter at people
my mind feels like a piece of furniture
flying back into the ethers
the only paradise I've ever found
reaches its final refrain
crossing the waters of Lake Pontchartrain

one hundred and forty-six
for Chris Champagne

I consider myself a ventriloquist of time & space
this castle comes perfectly heart-shaped
a wide flat river sits down in the room
put a candle between your eyes
turn in any direction
the truth is to see
if anything is beautiful or not
today I'm doing a floor puzzle with Mina
it's like fixing the chain on my first bicycle
I'm slipping you a note while I can
the news trickles out from a busted chronometer
my heart feels like an appendectomy
there isn't any place left to go

one hundred and forty-seven

tonite I'm amassing an enormous collection
of biology that says "I'm alive"
this is the tragedy of birth
consider the sky over New Orleans
during those weeks following the storm
you can't flip a coin
trying to reimagine a future
everything that's gone
goes on from a distance
that's why I am here
straining my eyes
to lay my hands on
the lush the depth of green

one hundred and forty-eight

for Joel Dailey

maybe there's a Walt Whitman in every backyard
and a dog eating grass
put on your finest robes
note the crepe myrtles' growth
measure it with your feet
choose any two of them
begin all over again
with sand in your shoes
sometimes it takes all day
this is what I wished for
I sing the colostrum the body epileptic
the magician's alphabet
is hard to undo

one hundred and forty-nine

for James Nolan

between half sleeping or half waking
my Mayan pocketwatch says
there's a whole galaxy
lit up with fireflies
where our ancestors evolve into trees
water can teach you many things
this one looks like a Chinese butterfly
the *I Ching* is another game of hide & seek
take the sun for example
at night during the day
summer goes by simple as a hello
it's obviously a well-planned affair
some say it's the moon

one hundred and fifty

the caveat onus is a song
whose silence reaches out in all directions
I have a hundred acre stare
I prefer the Hansel & Gretel method
I'm on the street
following my steps back down
the path I started from
tell me you're not talking to yourself
still here in ruins
often it's customary to have a smoke
at the end of anything
like the days themselves
I was just passing through

one hundred and fifty-one

for Lee Meitzen Grue

how many rabbit faces do you see
when the moon is nearly full
today I'm staring at childhood pictures
everything happens once many times
I have to sit two-dimensionally
the dog chases its tongue
infinity x 1 = ZZZzzzz
but let's begin first with laughter
or observing fireflies at close range
the evening Buddha flickers & reappears
I can see myself drawing
from elbow to ear
I'll even pretend this moment
    doesn't have a name

one hundred and fifty-two

a hurricane blows in from the south
I'm walking the levee with Megan Mina & Blaise
the waves coming up
are nearly invisible now
does amnesia shape the way you think
one must guess at a certain loneliness
$\longrightarrow$ children calling their mother
form a straight line from your mind to the sky
one for the piano one for the violin
mine was an improbable education not Cambridge
it's something I started doing one day
the universe likes playing ping pong with my eyes
I'm a monkey born like all the others

one hundred and fifty-three

for Daniel Kerwick

yesterday the voice on my knee said
rise up carcass and walk
your moon is cold
scarifications are an elegant gesture
at first I thought it was a practical joke
later we watched two pelicans
—> counting back to the hours of my birth
now I'm just glad there's a sky at all
take the sun for example
the light entering the holes in my head
is no longer a guess
my fingers feel like Edgar Allan Poe
this is a note of hello

one hundred and fifty-four

I should have guessed
my sleep is reckoned
beneath the feathers of a warm bird
below me is the most hated country in the world
and you can see it for miles
cities whose buildings are bent twisted back
    or gone
put a stethoscope to my chest
count backwards from 0 to 9
it's a prelude to a strange music
such eyes such pluck such fecund air
the horizon has clouds white and blue
and besides knowing what I knew
four rectangles a busted window the moon

one hundred and fifty-five

fill your mind with brackish water
this isn't an auditory hallucination
you are a ghost in splendid form
floating in the hallway
between the ceiling and the floor
swim in it as a sea now consumed
—> it's like moving dirt from one hole to another
and if my speech sounds untoward at times
I maintain an inevitability
to say I no longer wonder why
monkeys performed
question marks in my eyes
when I laugh I cry one by one

one hundred and fifty-six

comely I came dripping
with the scent of timeless stupid things
tearing pages from a book
the first chapter the best chapter
my vocabulary did this to me
I have no need to exist eternally
I was born under the serpent
church gives me a mustard feeling
the lizard ambles through leafy cover
I dress myself up in a hammock
   for the afternoon
a barge is making a wide turn downriver
the circumference of a circle
is a calendar that says August full moon

Coda

take the sun for example
I'm tying my shoes
to pretend everything has a purpose

turtle

one hundred and fifty-seven
for Helen Hill

in glimpses between two silent worlds
this is clear
skin fits tight to your bones
carrying a torch is a dim shadowy thing
the great killers of history
have hidden talents
I chase my light in buckets of black water
a girl in a blue dress
climbs a giant sunflower
the human silhouette drinks a cup of tea
most all of those I love
are the sound of footsteps
here surrounded by an inescapable serene

one hundred and fifty-eight

for Andrea Garland

have you ever watched a sundial
locate its shadow at the hour of noon
it's like an angel lying on its side
unaware of the time
or the hopelessness of the creatures
trapped under this sky
$\longrightarrow$ I will have an answer for everything one day
right now the cosmos of limbo
is barely noticeable
disappearing through the cracks of my eyes
as a thin slice of light
and the slight terror
that divides wakefulness from sleep

one hundred and fifty-nine

today's Mayan count reads
12 . 19 . 14 . 6 . 18   10 Etznab 6 Zotz
I feel like a zebra
at the beginning of the alphabet
lost in a dust cloud
on a crowded playground
O Huracán O Heart of the Sky
this is also known as the narrow road
to the interior
the Buddha of hello
the moon of full mind
I live below the river's edge
in the path of a Great Flood

one hundred and sixty

for Kemi Osundare

there are a thousand spectacles
in the caves of the jaw
the river unravels its tongue between the trees
will it be flow or flood
memory charts a path
water in your neighbor's front yard
—> shout these tidings
e jòwó e má ta yèpè si o
in the Word was the Beginning
to utter is to alter
one silver eye in a magnitude of ripples
breaking walls walls breaking
like a tyrant for his noose

" In the beginning was the Word ... "

John 1:1

one hundred and sixty-one

Brenda Coultas

as a traveler on my toes
I adore routine
in polite monosyllables
curious lights in the skies over earth
like planets Venus or Mercury
help me to my destination
handsomely each morning
I inscribe my mind on an elaborate scroll
even when ghost-like appurtenances
transform my appearance
it's a small certainty
why anything is possible
my smile has no cure

one hundred and sixty-two

whatever is treason
but the account of a nation
that treats its citizens like pigs & dogs
those who cannot remember the future
are condemned to repeat it
from the scratching of mice
to the howler monkey
the clock stops at the precise hour
the heartfelt defense of Charlie Chaplin
that was the beginning of the word "hope"
fire and water are the same thing
eating the noise of grasshoppers
there are no lost steps

one hundred and sixty-three

in an older younger age
would the trees praise us
for our good behavior
rest your head
on a bed of feathers
this is your secret hour
what you came for
but to disappear entirely
that is a rare gift
passing through this shadow world
neither living nor dead
so tell it all
there's much work to do

one hundred and sixty-four

a book is waiting to be written
its light is a glimmer which knows no origin
its glance dances from the prow
of a crystal ship
transcribing a flickering weather
under the sign of wonder
—> who would rather die than kill
but to say the moon is a dangerous weapon
this is the song of time
as turtle calls its legs and head
back to its shell
that ungentle balance between fate and men
hanging slow-motioned in the breeze

one hundred and sixty-five

I have a trembling urge to moan
like the statues at the wax museum
the other me feels
like a funeral marching
across a shadowy plain
it's a math that understands
the distant present
tiny spirals form
at the back of the mind
occasionally life comes
to a grinding halt
the miracle is straightforward
toxic gases a sulfuric stench

one hundred and sixty-six

the outbreak of war has no season
like deer or other wild game
some soldiers
pull the trigger on their enemies
so many times
they develop calluses
→ on their forefinger and thumb
thus as the commander-in-chief takes aim
at the next military campaign
   in the Middle East
another cortege makes its way
o'er the land
followed by a chaplain
a mother and her son

one hundred and sixty-seven

I'm waiting for the moon to pass
ballroom-gowned
at the rear of a parade
I am the feelinglessness of sepulchre
the weather of flambeaux
a songsheet composed from human detritus
skipping elegantly over your grave
on quiet clear nights my eyes
pay homage to a path of shiny footprints
forming an arc across the sky
here lies a new leviathan
the body was not built for perfection
I can only imagine the smell of its dying brain

one hundred and sixty-eight

for Ed and Miriam Sanders

I can't leave you unexpectedly
but you know I will
beneath a dazzling rain
all the joys of twisting & wandering
a path overgrown with glowing oaks
sewn into the palm
⟶> which mouth will you choose
the Egret the Ibis the Great Blue Heron
dear friend I'm unlocking the door
here's a fresh supply of linens
you are inside the *Grand Hôtel de l'Univers*
a pigmy blasting his molimo trumpet
into the void

one hundred and sixty-nine

for Bill Warren and Pati D'Amico

all days become nocturnes
when hurricane season begins
check the list at City Hall
for the houses scheduled for demolition
what will the 82nd Airborne
save us from the next time
they arrive and the city is empty
a recent FBI report says New Orleans
is the murder capital of America
and apart from the lies
I hold to be self-evident
listen carefully dear reader
there is but one dark truth

Notes on the Text

The Cycle. *The Caveat Onus* is cyclical poem of meditations based on the numerical value of thirteen, with each meditation consisting of thirteen lines, and with each section containing thirteen meditations; and the entire work being comprised of thirteen sections in all.

The Composition. I began writing *Book One* of *The Caveat Onus* in mid-December 2004. It was fully my intention to take my time with it, but those circumstances changed. As such, I completed *Book Three* in November 2006, with the final thirteen meditations, *Coda*, following shortly thereafter.

Hexagrams. One of the operations of this work is that each meditation should function loosely as a hexagram, actually two hexagrams (the first six lines and the last six lines); thus leaving the middle line (the seventh line) to serve as a kind of spine, or as I would like to think, an axis mundi, the center of a sphere, with a line moving through that point in space, in both directions.

The Delineation. Each section begins with a totem animal. Each totem animal directly corresponds to the Bak'tun Cycle of the Mayan Calendar where the solar year is divided into thirteen moons rather than twelve months.

The Symmetry of Sonnegrams. The thirteen-line form throughout *The Caveat Onus*, the sonnegram, is a form which I conceived specifically for this work. It creates a peculiar matrix with regards to the readings of each meditation. Often, and very clearly, the meditations can be considered as follows: first line – last line; second line – second to last line; third line – third to last line; and so on, moving inward, until one reaches the final line, which is the seventh line. In addition, this symmetry provides for the converse to be true as well, beginning with the seventh line, then moving outward.

The Matrix. The matrix reaches its most distilled form in the final section of each book (*owl, hawk, rabbit*) wherein a complete expurgation of my theories on chance methodologies, double-helix intuitions, numerical gyroscopes and shamanistic connections is fully drawn upon and simultaneously employed. In fact, the final section of each book can be considered as two giant hexagrams (the first six meditations and the last six meditations) with the middle meditation serving as the overall central axis, and most literally, the vanishing point for each book.

Vanishing Points. My understanding of vanishing point is that point on a physical plane, for example, in the works of Leonardo da Vinci, where everything disappears. Alternately, my understanding of vanishing point has a very specific frame of reference directly corresponding to quantum mechanics; and, in this context, can be described simply as that irreducible point in space where zero mass can be found.

Architectonics of the Work. *Notes on the Text* is intended to provide an entry to the overall structure of *The Caveat Onus* and thereby does not presuppose to be a summation of its parts.

Postscript. The circumstances as to why this work wrote itself so quickly have a lot to do with the evening of 28 August 2005; when it became apparent that the eye of the hurricane was going to come ashore and move almost directly over New Orleans. After that night, due to the inundations of land by water spanning a period of several weeks, the only significant light that New Orleans would experience after sundown came from the moon. And just as the moon is the guiding principle of water, so it is with this work.

D.B. 29.viii.08

Born in 1967 and raised in New Orleans, Dave Brinks is the editor of *YAWP: A Journal of Poetry & Art*, publisher of Trembling Pillow Press, director of 17 Poets! Literary & Performance Series, poetry editor for *ArtVoices* magazine, and founder of the New Orleans School for the Imagination and New Orleans Artists Guild. His poetry has been published in dozens of magazines, newspapers, journals, and anthologies throughout the U.S., Canada, and overseas. His works also have aired on NPR's *All Things Considered* and PBS' *NewsHour with Jim Lehrer*, and have been featured in *National Geographic Traveler* and *Louisiana Cultural Vistas*. His poetry collections include *The Snow Poems* (Lavender Ink 2000), *The Treehouse Aquarium Cathedral Room* (with Bernadette Mayer, New Directions 2005), *The Caveat Onus: Book One, Book Two, Book Three,* and *Coda* (Lavender Ink 2006, 2007), *The Science of Forgetting* (with Bernadette Mayer, Trembling Pillow Press 2009), *The Light on Earth Street, How Birds Fly, The Secret Brain, The Wilderness of Things,* and *A Pot of Lips* (Lavender Ink 2009). Brinks is currently at work on *The Geometry of Sound,* an experimental and cross-disciplinary, book-length poem that explores the origins of alphabets & writing systems.

TITLES FROM BLACK WIDOW PRESS

TRANSLATION SERIES

Chanson Dada: Selected Poems
by Tristan Tzara
Translated with an introduction and essay
by Lee Harwood.

Approximate Man and Other Writings
by Tristan Tzara
Translated and edited by Mary Ann Caws.

Poems of André Breton:
A Bilingual Anthology
Translated with essays by Jean-Pierre
Cauvin and Mary Ann Caws.

Last Love Poems of Paul Eluard
Translated with an introduction by
Marilyn Kallet.

Capital of Pain by Paul Eluard
Translated by Mary Ann Caws, Patricia
Terry, and Nancy Kline.

Love, Poetry (L'amour la poésie)
by Paul Eluard
Translated with an essay by Stuart Kendall.

The Sea and Other Poems by Guillevic
Translated by Patricia Terry. Introduction
by Monique Chefdor.

Essential Poems and Writings of
Robert Desnos: A Bilingual Anthology
Edited with an introduction and essay
by Mary Ann Caws.

Essential Poems and Writings of
Joyce Mansour: A Bilingual Anthology
Translated with an introduction by
Serge Gavronsky.

Poems of A.O. Barnabooth
by Valery Larbaud
Translated by Ron Padgett and
Bill Zavatsky.

EyeSeas (Les Ziaux)
by Raymond Queneau
Translated with an introduction by
Daniela Hurezanu and Stephen Kessler.

To Speak, to Tell You? by Sabine Sicaud
Translated by Norman R. Shapiro. Intro-
duction and notes by Odile Ayral-Clause.

Art Poétique by Guillevic
Translated by Maureen Smith.

forthcoming translations

Furor and Mystery and Other Writings
by René Char
Edited and translated by Mary Ann Caws
and Nancy Kline.

La Fontaine's Bawdy
by Jean de la Fontaine
Translated with an introduction by
Norman R. Shapiro.

Inventor of Love & Other Writings
by Ghérasim Luca
Translated by Julian and Laura Semilian.
Introduction by Andrei Codrescu. Essay
by Petre Răileanu.

The Big Game by Benjamin Péret
Translated with an introduction by
Marilyn Kallet.

I Want No Part in It and Other Writings
by Benjamin Péret
Translated with an introduction by
James Brook.

Essential Poems and Writings
of Jules Laforgue
Translated and edited by Patricia Terry.

Preversities: A Jacques Prévert Sampler
Translated and edited by Norman R.
Shapiro.

Essential Poems and Writings
of Pierre Reverdy
Translated by Mary Ann Caws and
Patricia Terry.

MODERN POETRY SERIES

An Alchemist with One Eye on Fire
by Clayton Eshleman

Archaic Design by Clayton Eshleman

Backscatter: New and Selected Poems
by John Olson

Crusader-Woman
by Ruxandra Cesereanu
Translated by Adam J. Sorkin.
Introduction by Andrei Codrescu.

The Grindstone of Rapport:
A Clayton Eshleman Reader
Forty years of poetry, prose, and
translations by Clayton Eshleman.

Packing Light: New and Selected Poems
by Marilyn Kallet

Forgiven Submarine by Ruxandra
Cesereanu and Andrei Codrescu

The Caveat Onus by Dave Brinks
The complete cycle, four vols. in one.

forthcoming modern poetry titles

Fire Exit by Robert Kelly

Concealments and Caprichos
by Jerome Rothenberg

Anticline by Clayton Eshleman

Larynx Galaxy by John Olson

NEW POETS SERIES

Signal from Draco: New and Selected Poems
by Mebane Robertson

LITERARY THEORY/BIOGRAPHY SERIES

Revolution of the Mind:
The Life of André Breton
by Mark Polizzotti
Revised and augmented edition.

WWW.BLACKWIDOWPRESS.COM

Colophon

This text was set in Adobe Caslon Pro. Caslon is a serif typeface designed by William Caslon I (1692–1766); this variant was designed by Carol Twombly in 1990. Characterized by short ascenders and descenders, bracketed serifs, and a moderate stroke, Caslon was the first original typeface of English origin and distributed throughout the British Empire, including British North America. Caslon's types were used in many historic documents. The titling font is Caslon Antique, a decorative serif typeface originally called Fifteenth Century.